So Many Beeps in This House

Copyright © 2024 by Nancy Udell

All rights reserved.

In accordance with the U.S. Copyright Act of 1976, the scanning, uploading and electronic sharing of any part of this book without the permission of the publisher is unlawful piracy and theft of the author's intellectual property. If you would like to use material from the book (other than for review purposes), prior written permission must be obtained by contacting the publisher.

Published in the United States by

Publishing Division
P.O. Box 2884
Pawleys Island, SC 29585
www.ClassAtPawleys.com

Story and illustrations by Nancy Udell
Illustrations based on photographs by Treycen McLeod

ISBN 978-1-955095-38-9

Printed in the U.S.A.

Dedication

To my darling grandsons,
Marco, the enthusiastic beep hunter,
and
Treycen, the intrepid photographer.
Thank you for all the joy and laughter
you bring into my life. I love you.

Once upon a time, Nana moved to Florida to be near her family, including her two wonderful grandsons, Treycen and Marco.

Nana loved her new house in Florida and was so happy to be near her family.

But there was one thing about the new house that was hard for Nana to get used to.

It had so many beeps!

Beeps that Nana had never heard before.

One day, Nana and Marco were hanging out at Nana's new house when all of a sudden ...

beep! beep! beep!

"What was that beeping, Nana?"

"Oh bunny," Nana sighed. "There are so many beeps in this house."

"So many beeps in this house!" said Marco.
Marco loved to repeat.

"Maybe it's the oven," Nana said. "Are our cookies done?"

Nana and Marco had put a batch of cookies in the oven not long ago.

"Cookies!" cried Marco. Nana and Marco walked over to the oven to check the timer.

They were about to open the oven and look at the cookies when . . .

beep! beep! beep!

"Still beeping, Nana!" Marco said.

"So many beeps in this house!" they said together, laughing.

"Maybe it's the dryer!" said Nana after a pause.

"Maybe it's the dryer!" said Marco.

Nana and Marco walked down into the laundry room. They looked at the dryer.

The dryer was still going round and round.
It was making a warm bumping noise.

They looked inside just in case.
The warm damp clothes settled to the bottom.

But no beeps.

"Nope, not the dryer!" Nana said.

"Not the dryer!" Marco echoed exuberantly.

And at that moment...

beep! beep! beep!

Nana and Marco look at each other and shouted happily...

"So many beeps in this house!"

They settled down again, thinking about the beeps.

"Let me see," said Nana. She was almost at a loss.

"Wait," she said, "maybe it's the smoke detector?"

"What's a smoke detector, Nana?" asked Marco.

"Well, it's a little machine that tells us if there is smoke in house. Do you see it up there?" she said, pointing. "It beeps when the batteries get low."

Nana got out
the stool.

They both climbed
up to check the
batteries.

And just as they
were looking ...
from a
　　　completely
　　　　　different
　　　　　　　direction,
they heard...

beep!
beep! beep!

"Not the smoke detector,"
Nana said balefully.

"Not the smoke detector,"
Marco said jubilantly.

"SO MANY BEEPS IN
THIS HOUSE!"
they said together,
laughing.

"Ok," said Nana,
"it's not the oven."

"And it's not the dryer,"
said Marco.

"And it's not the smoke
detector," said Nana.

Nana thought.

Marco listened hard.

"Wait," Nana said. "Maybe it's the dishwasher! It beeps when it's done."

"Maybe it's the dishwasher," Marco echoed excitedly.

But alas, as they went into the kitchen, the very silent dishwasher stared back at them.

Then, a certain familiar sound came just from over Nana's shoulder. . .

beep!

beep!

beep!

And they realized . . .

"It's the fridge!" shouted Nana.

"It's the fridge!" yelled Marco, throwing his hands in the air.

The doors of the fridge were slightly open.

"I guess we didn't close it all the way when we got out the ingredients for the cookies!" Nana said.

Nana and Marco pushed the fridge doors closed with a sense of satisfaction.

Thunk!

Finally!

"I never had a fridge that beeped before," said Nana. "My goodness!"

And then ... *Beep! Beep! Beep!*

"WHAT???" said Marco.

"Wait a minute!" said Nana.

They looked at each other.

"The cookies!" they said together, laughing.

Indeed, the new beep was coming from the oven, the very first place they had checked.

"So many beeps in this house!" They said once again. They could not help laughing.

And, the cookies were done!

Nana and Marco sat down to a well deserved plate of nice warm cookies and two glasses of cold milk.

They made sure to close the fridge securely!

Nana's new house was strangely silent, except for their happy chatter. The beeping was at rest for the moment.

"I love you, bunny," Nana said. "You are the best person to find beeps with!"

"I love you, too, Nana," Marco said.

"Well," said Nana, when they finished their snack, "time to go home."

"OK Nana," Marco said, eyeing the plate of the cookies.

Nana wrapped the rest of the cookies in wax paper for Marco to take home.

Marco put the package in his backpack.

Nana and Marco headed for the car. They got in and Nana started the engine. All of a sudden …

BEEP! BEEP! BEEP!

"Your seatbelt!" said Nana.

"SO MANY BEEPS IN THIS CAR," they said together, laughing.

Then … *ding!*

"Text message," Nana said, holding up her phone, still laughing.

And off they went.

The End

www.ingramcontent.com/pod-product-compliance
Lightning Source LLC
Chambersburg PA
CBHW041408010526
44107CB00015B/1112